Building a Small Cable Suspension Bridge
with the Cable Locking System

Marvin Denmark
Robin Koontz

MADENMARK

Madenmark Publishing
PO Box 484
Noti, OR 97461

10 9 8 7 6 5 4 3 2 1

Copyright © 2011 by Marvin Denmark and Robin Koontz
All rights reserved, including the right of reproduction in whole or in part in any form without permission in writing from the publisher, except by a reviewer who may quote brief passages in a review.

ISBN-13: 978-0615438139 (Madenmark Publishing)
ISBN-10: 061543813X

Book design by Robin Koontz
Illustrations by Marvin Denmark
Photographs by Robin Koontz except where noted

Library of Congress Cataloging-in-Publication Data
Denmark, Marvin Koontz, Robin
Building a Small Cable Suspension Bridge with the Cable Locking System /
Marvin Denmark and Robin Koontz

*dedicated to the desire
to create something interesting*

Contents

Acknowledgements	VII
Disclaimer	VIII
Chapter 1 Why a Bridge?	1
Chapter 2 A Little History	7
Chapter 3 How it Works	13
Chapter 4 Finding the Right Site	19
Chapter 5 The Posts	23
Chapter 6 Curves and Gallops	27
Chapter 7 The Final Design	31
Chapter 8 Getting Started	35

Chapter 9 Setting the Posts	39
Chapter 10 Collars and Backfill	43
Chapter 11 The Dead-Men	49
Chapter 12 The Cables	55
Chapter 13 The Assembly	63
Chapter 14 Decking and Details	69
Chapter 15 The Patent	73
Materials List	76
Chronological List of Events	77
Afterwords	78

VI

Acknowledgements

Many thanks to everyone in our family and friend circle who have encouraged, applauded, and contributed to the first Funny Farm bridge project. We also thank Ray Cook and Rudy Berg for their engineering expertise. Special thanks to Doug, our longtime friend, who has always cleared his calendar to help out with the projects and share a few donuts and beers, though not at the same time.

Furry thanks to all of our critters, past and present. This is Mollie, our shortest and most critical supervisor.

Disclaimer

This is a "how we did it" book about our experience building a small cable suspension bridge on our property in western Oregon. We do not claim that the information is complete or that the methods and materials we used will meet engineering and/or building requirements. For example, after engineering review, it was determined that the dead men should have been heavier to deal with longevity creep in movable soils and potential future loading.

Anyone who wants to use this book as a guide for building a small cable suspension bridge should check into permits and building codes in their area and consider having their bridge design engineered.

Further, we have no control over how the reader chooses to use what he or she learns from the information in our book, and we have no idea about the reader's level of competence or their sites' physical conditions. Therefore, we are not responsible for any mishaps or problems that might occur as a result of using information found in this book.

We do hope that you get good ideas and inspiration, and that you enjoy our bridge building journey!

Chapter 1

Why a Bridge?

We are fortunate to own about 55 acres of property in a little valley that is nestled in the eastern side of the Coast Range Mountains of Oregon.

The property has about 3/4 mile of creek running through it. While it's a peaceful and cool place to hang out in the hot summer, this creek can become a large torrent during the winter rainy season, making it virtually impossible to cross safely.

2 BUILDING A SMALL CABLE SUSPENSION BRIDGE

There was usually little reason for us to cross the creek in the winter, except for the fact that our farm's water supply is spring-fed, and the spring is located across the creek and up a mountain. Spring systems are usually okay if left alone, but we sometimes have issues.

The plastic pipe from the spring to our house runs above ground through the woods. Trees and branches sometimes fall and cause damage. Animals such as deer and elk sometimes puncture holes in the pipe with their sharp hooves. We have also had a bear visitor who liked to rip apart the covering structure, allowing leaves and other debris to clog up the system.

A black bear caught with a Stealth Cam wildlife motion camera.

The bear would also pull out the filter system and chomp holes in the waterline, overall making a mess of things when he was in the mood. We finally installed a battery-charged electric fence around the spring to keep him out of it, but the other issues were still unpredictable and regular, especially during the stormy winters.

It seemed a good idea to have an easy way to get across the creek in winter. And it would also open up more areas for us to hike and plant trees along the creek bank.

Railroad flatcar bridge on a neighboring property.

Our fantasy was to bring in a steel railroad car and construct a road bridge across the creek. We got as far as lining up the purchase of an old flatcar for a reasonable price and talking to crane operators. However, when the dollar amounts and permit requirements for such a huge undertaking became daunting, we sacked the idea, for now anyway.

Marvin decided to design and build a footbridge. Marvin, who designs and builds other unique structures, determined that a suspension style bridge would serve the purpose very well. And it would look pretty cool spanning across the creek, too.

He began futzing in his shop, coming up with ideas for the design. In pondering the act of constructing the bridge and ideas to make it logistically easier, Marvin came up with a unique way to put it all together without needing to be in the creek for the assembly.

Marvin invented a fairly simple contraption that would allow easy on-site installation. Thanks to this invention, all of the spanning bridge parts could be built on dry land and assembled and if necessary, replaced, pretty much "on the fly."

The Cable-Locking System doing its job

Before construction even began, we applied for a utility patent on Marvin's idea which we called the Cable Locking System. We were surprised to find out that no one had patented anything like it! Once our patent was pending, we proceeded with the bridge construction. The entire building process took about six months, but only because Marvin was also working on other projects for pay at the time and was busy with other farm tasks. Otherwise, this bridge could have been done in a few weekends.

I took movies and photos, sometimes turning my head so I didn't have to look at some of the precarious tasks. While not the right job for the unbalanced, Marvin's patent-pending locking system worked like a charm. Once the parts were constructed and the foundation was in place, it was only a few days before we could walk across our new bridge.

What follows is the story of building this bridge. This is not a "how to" book, as we have no intention of telling anyone how to build a bridge. Instead, this is a "how we did it" book. We'll go through every step of the process that produced this particular suspension bridge.

You can get ideas from this design and derive some helpful hints about how to put it all together. The design illustration with call-outs is included for reference, but you are more than welcome to use it. Information for having us manufacture parts for the cable locking system is at the end of this book.

Chapter 2

A Little History

The first known suspension bridges were made of natural materials such as vines, rope, sticks and wood planks. Chains were also used in the construction of some suspension bridges. These fairly easy to build bridges were a pretty easy way to get people across difficult to traverse terrains and waterways.

This bridge in Singapore possibly started out with ropes for suspenders, then cable and chain were added to keep it out of the water.

Photo by Pavol Kmeto/ Shutterstock.com

Usually they were used as footbridges. Many of us have tried out one of these "swinging bridges" at a park or other remote or primitive location.

Kazura Vine Suspension Bridge over the Iya-gawa River in Shikoku, Japan.

148 feet (45 meters) long, this bridge is a national important folkloric property as one of Japan's three rare bridges. The bridge is rebuilt every three years.

Photo courtesy of Richard Farmer

But soon, suspension bridges were built wide enough and strong enough to safely bring across animals and carts. It's fun to imagine the process of building one of these early bridges. It's also fun to imagine convincing the cattle and sheep to cross these swinging structures.

In more modern times, engineers figured out that a suspension bridge design could span great distances using fewer materials and labor compared to stone, post/pier or other tried bridge designs. Meanwhile as people built cities and sprawled into bigger spaces of land, the need for an easy access and shortcuts across rivers and gorges inspired a lot of new bridge designs.

Japan is the current owner of the world's longest central span suspension bridge. The Akashi-Kaikyo Bridge, also called the Pearl Bridge, is 6,532 feet (1,991 meters) long. Photo by Laitr Keiows/Shutterstock.com

A suspension bridge had a sleek and elegant appearance, and it could span extremely long distances for less time and materials. It soon became one of the more popular modern bridge designs.

Today, suspension bridges are the longest spanning structures in the world, often serving as the best solution for crossing deep water channels where installing supporting piers is not easy and very costly. Dollar per foot, suspension bridges are typically less expensive to build. And they are cool looking!

10 BUILDING A SMALL CABLE SUSPENSION BRIDGE

The suspension bridge design has not been without problems, primarily due to lack of structural engineering knowledge and/or attempts to cut costs in the materials and construction. The famous Tacoma Narrows Bridge in Washington State went down in history as the one of the worst engineering disasters in history.

A multitude of problems caused its 1940 collapse about four months after it opened, including wind-induced "harmonic resonance." This resonance is now considered less of a reason for the bridge's collapse than was the width to length ratio of the bridge deck plus the lack of stiffening trusses.

The Tacoma Narrows Bridge, aka Galloping Gertie, was the third longest suspension bridge in the world when it opened, with a suspended length of about 5,000 feet (1524 meters).

Photo courtesy of Kenneth J. Zajac

Bridge model in a wind test, reacting to 90 meters per second (about 200 miles per hour) of wind velocity.

Photographer unknown

Wind was definitely a factor in the collapse of the Tacoma Narrows Bridge, and since then all bridge designs proposed in the U.S. have to go through stringent aerodynamic studies before being approved for construction.

Engineers are also developing sonar sensors that may be able to detect cracks long before they can cause any problems in bridge construction. They will be able to send sound waves into steel and analyze the returning waves for changes in pitch, which can signal hidden cracks and other defects.

12 BUILDING A SMALL CABLE SUSPENSION BRIDGE

The Silver Bridge after its collapse in 1967.

Photo courtesy of the Point Pleasant River Museum, Point Pleasant, West Virginia.

The Silver Bridge was constructed in 1928 between Point Pleasant, West Virginia and Kanauga, Ohio. It collapsed on December 15, 1967, causing 46 deaths. It was the first suspension bridge to hang from a linked chain of steel bars instead of wire cables. A crack formed within one of the links, and that link along with the chain snapped, plunging the bridge into the Ohio River.

As a result of the Silver Bridge disaster, the National Bridge Inspection Standard (NBIS) was created.

Suspension bridge at Saint-Denis-de-Pile after its collapse in 1931.

Photo by Jeanne Vacher

Chapter 3

How It Works

There are basically two types of cable suspension bridges. In the A-shape design, cables are run from the deck up to a post or tower where they are secured. The load forces are primarily on the vertical posts and on the bridge deck. This is called a cable-stayed bridge.

This A-Style suspension bridge across the Corinth Gulf strait, Greece is the world's second longest cable-stayed bridge.
Photo by ollirg/Shutterstock.com

14 BUILDING A SMALL CABLE SUSPENSION BRIDGE

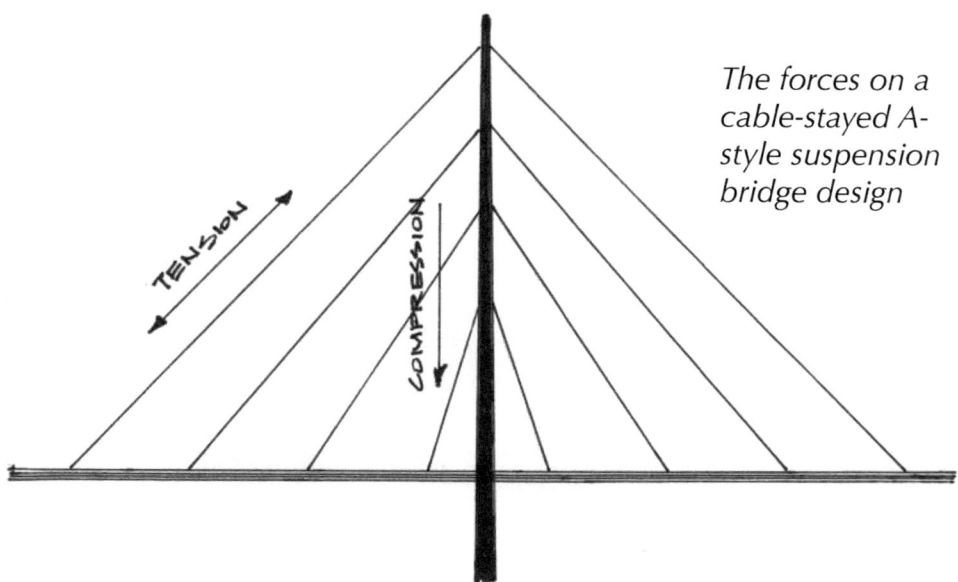

The forces on a cable-stayed A-style suspension bridge design

In the M-shape suspension bridge style, the cables are positioned into a convex arch and anchored securely at each end of the span after passing over the end posts. Hangers or suspenders span from the cables down to the deck system. In this design, the cables and the four anchor points help to carry much of the load-bearing job of the posts.

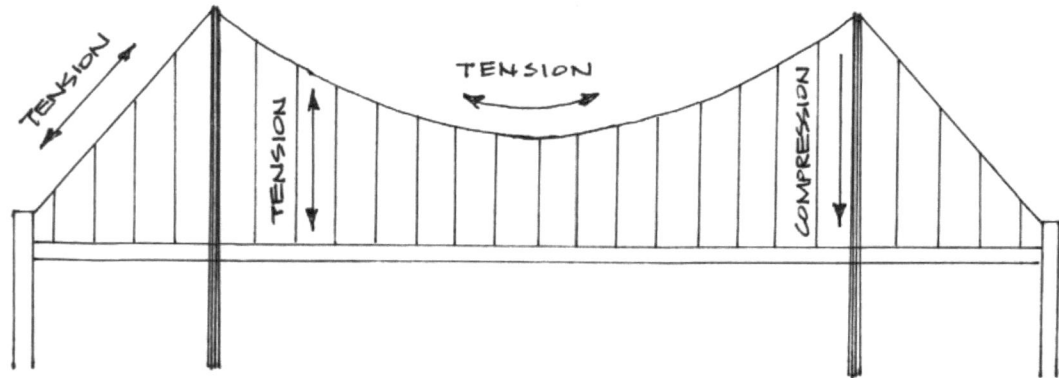

The forces on an M-style suspension bridge design

The Golden Gate Bridge in San Francisco is an M-style suspension bridge.
Photo by Jon Sullivan

Our bridge is more of the M-style suspension bridge. For a small-scale foot bridge, Marvin was not too concerned about width vs. length, but he was definitely concerned about the anchoring points, stability of the posts, cable strength, resonance, deck material, trusses, and the catenary curve of the two main cables.

16 BUILDING A SMALL CABLE SUSPENSION BRIDGE

The catenary curve is the curve assumed by a heavy uniform flexible cord hanging freely from two points. The curve of the main cables will evenly distribute the weight of the deck among all of the suspenders, which are the cables that run from the main cables to the deck assembly. The curve also determines the relative lengths of all the suspenders.

The St. Louis Gateway Arch is built in the shape of an upside-down catenary curve. Photo by HHsu/Shutterstock.com

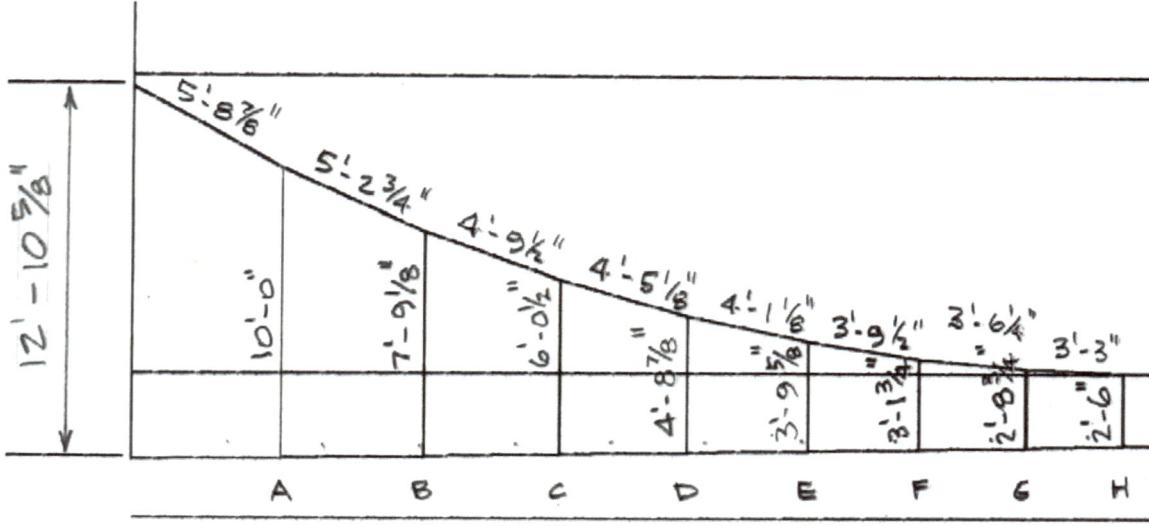

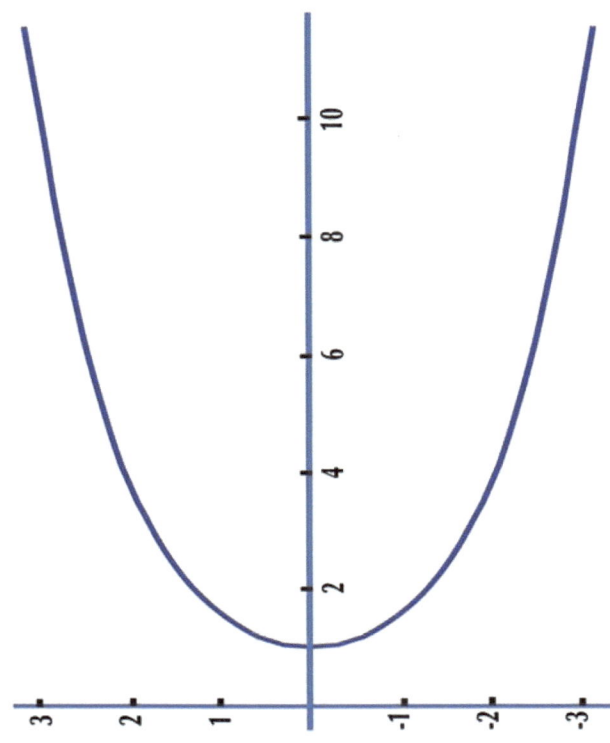

The catenary is the curve formed by a perfectly flexible inextensible chain of uniform density that is hanging from two supports

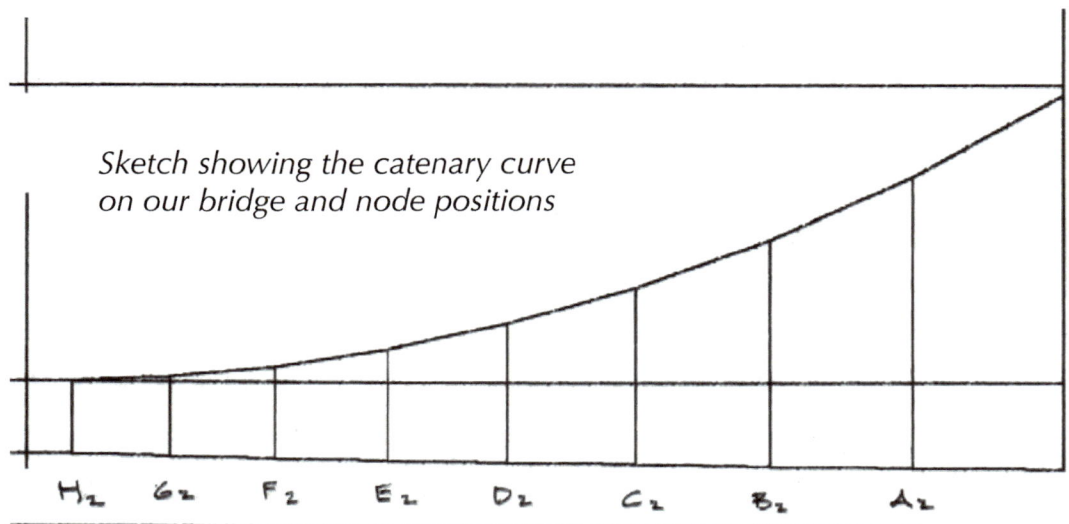

Sketch showing the catenary curve on our bridge and node positions

18 BUILDING A SMALL CABLE SUSPENSION BRIDGE

View of the bridge during high water. It is so much nicer than swimming across the creek in January!

Marvin had to figure out how the cables were going to curve in the most efficient and eye-pleasing manner to support the structure while still looking cool. Once he knew the length of the bridge and the height of the towers, it was a matter of deciding the depth of the curve of the cables to the deck of the bridge. Before all of that could be decided, Marvin needed to pick out the bridge site.

Chapter 4

Finding the Right Site

The perfect bridge site would have the same elevation on both sides of the space and landing areas that are well out of the flood hazard, as much as possible. Marvin didn't worry much about length since a suspension bridge can span a long way, but he did keep it in mind as he explored all the possibilities. Naturally, our goal was to have the bridge land close to the path to the spring, but there were other considerations.

Marvin used a transit level to check elevations on either side of the creek.

The site also needed to have good soil or rock to support the anchor points. Since these points were going to be the integral part of the bridge's support system, a predominantly sandy soil would not be easy to form for the depth needed, and we have pretty sandy soil closer to the creek. So that meant backing pretty far off the bank for the anchor points. We traveled up and down the creek, looking for just the right spot for our bridge.

The little waterfall between the trees is run-off from the spring up the hill.

The width of the creek in summer was about 40 feet across at this point.

Marvin settled on a site that was fairly clear and level on both sides and, both sides were at about the same elevation.

The area for the posts had a soil mixture of clay and sand which would be fairly easy to work and would hold its shape. The area was about twenty feet from the creek bank at high water on either side. There was plenty of space behind the post locations for those vital anchor points.

Another consideration was the large debris that floated downstream during high water. Many times we have seen chunks of trees and large branches riding the tide at close to 20 miles per hour. Having the deck low on the water could mean some of that stuff could get tangled up in the bridge.

Marvin decided to suspend the deck about two feet off the ground and therefore would be suspended well above the high-water mark, allowing debris to float underneath. He would build a small stair with a landing on either side. The stair landings would be portable so if we had serious high-water warnings, we could toss them into a flood-safe area.

We also liked the spot because there was only some brush to clear for the foundation. Digging wasn't easy (all done by hand) but at least there were no horrific roots and boulders to deal with and we had that good workable soil.

Marvin used metal stakes and string to help measure lengths and determine elevation. A transit level came in handy for this chore, too. Another site that we liked would have required building up on one side to keep the bridge level, requiring a lot of stairs or a steep ramp to get up and down on one side. We also liked that it was a good landing point to get to the spring.

One of many log jams in the creek. They can break loose during high-water and damage a bridge that hangs low, but are good for spawning fish.

Chapter 5

The Posts

The posts as well as the length of the deck were going to determine the design of this bridge. We had purchased 4″ square tube steel posts to use for the bridge supports. However, Marvin opted not to use them. They would have had to be pre-drilled (1/4 inch thick metal needs a drill press), since drilling on site with a cordless drill standing on a ladder seemed too difficult. The holes for the cable and deck assemblies needed to be lined up perfectly on either side of the creek, not off to one side or the other, or there would be wearing from stress down the road. The precision that would have been required to line everything up when setting up the posts would have been cumbersome. Marvin had another option for the posts.

We still have the square tube steel posts. They are waiting around for another project.

24 BUILDING A SMALL CABLE SUSPENSION BRIDGE

We belong to an electric co-op. They give a power pole about 35 years before they come in and replace it, that is, unless something happens sooner such as insect infestation and subsequent woodpecker damage. Most of the discarded poles still have plenty of life in them; they just no longer meet pretty stringent power pole standards. Marvin decided to use power poles instead of the steel, for the reasons already mentioned.

We have acquired a few nice power poles over the years and have made good use of them. We learned from a farmer in Stayton, Oregon that barb wire makes a great bird nesting-box hanging device. The barbs keep the houses from sliding into each other and cavity-dwelling birds that we have here such as swallows, bluebirds, chickadees and wrens love the hanging habitats.

Marvin is tightening up the hanging nest-box wire before the birds come back in spring. There is a power pole on either end of the line.

Tree swallow babies waiting for someone to come and feed them

Marvin determined that we didn't need the entire 30' post for the bird box hangers, so he got out the chain saw and cut 15 feet out of each one. The birds never noticed.

Marvin had another power pole that we hadn't used yet and got two more solid 15 foot sections out of it. He figured about three feet in the ground plus two feet from the deck to the ground would give him about ten feet of height from cable to deck. We also knew from our ground plan that the bridge deck was going to be about 80 feet long. So two known factors were in place for the design. One to go.

Chapter 6

Curves and Gallops

The next thing to figure out is the catenary curve. The factors to consider for the curve can get complicated. There truly is a mathematical formula to get the "ideal" weight load distribution in a curve. The engineers call that ideal an "equal resistance catenary." This is when the cable's resistance to breaking is equal along its entire length. To accomplish this bit of perfection, we consulted my brother the engineer. He was a great help in getting a better understanding of the physics behind catenary curves.

Catenary comes from the Latin word catena, meaning "chain."

28 BUILDING A SMALL CABLE SUSPENSION BRIDGE

The Catenary

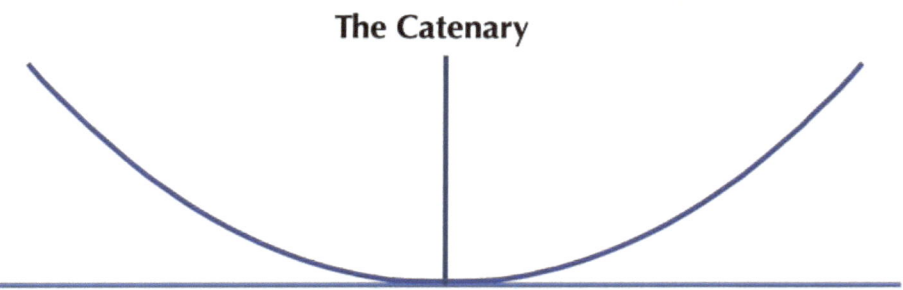

Marvin also implemented a hands-on string method for determining his catenary curve for the bridge design. He mocked up our bridge by creating a scale model. This way, he could draw up the posts and deck at the pre-determined height and length, respectively, then he set the catenary curve to his liking by using pins and heavy nylon fishing line. He could double-check using the math, but it was nice to have something physical that could be adjusted.

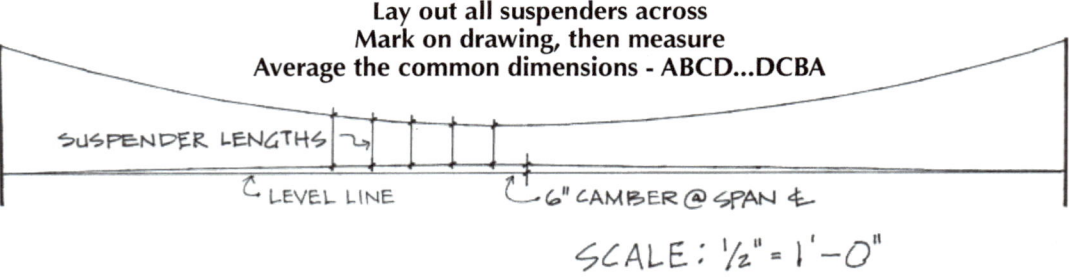

This approach at determining the catenary, though being less precise than the mathematical one, can be used to solve undetermined configurations.

After the degree of the curve was calculated and fixed on the model, Marvin drew in the suspenders and recorded the lengths. He would wind up with something like "ABCDDCBA" where the suspenders on each end were the same length and the longest, and then coming toward center of the next two on either end a little shorter, and so on. However, they were not spaced equally. Why not?

To Gallop or Not to Gallop?

While harmonic resonance was not completely to blame for the failure of Galloping Gertie, Marvin decided to address the problem because it could be an issue. After all, the bridge was bound to be a little bouncy, so why make it worse?

All objects have a frequency or a set of frequencies with which they will naturally resonate when disturbed in some way - be it plucking a guitar or stepping on a bridge deck. Each of these natural frequencies is associated with a wave pattern. When the object resonates at one of its natural frequencies, it vibrates in a manner so that a standing wave is formed within the confines of the object.

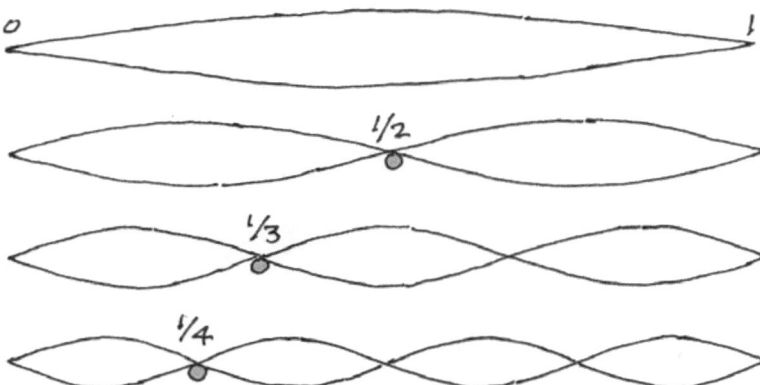

A set of standing waves, in a "container" of a specific length. This set of waves is called a harmonic series, the grey dots are the nodes.

Harmonic resonance refers to the multiples of the strongest resonance of, in this case, a mechanical system. Resonance is the tendency of the system to absorb more energy when its oscillations match the system's natural frequency of vibration. Resonance can cause swaying motions, but there are ways to reduce those motions. Since this was just an 80-foot long bridge, resonance was not a serious concern, but Marvin decided to use one trick to prevent it from waving "on its nodes."

30 BUILDING A SMALL CABLE SUSPENSION BRIDGE

In the case of resonance for this bridge, the waves will bounce back and forth between two boundaries: the posts. Nodes are always at equally spaced intervals where the wave amplitude (motion) is zero. The points where the cable connects to the post are two nodes. There is a possibility for one node in the middle, at third points, at quarter points, and so on, as seen in the previous drawing showing standing waves. The more excitation, the more nodes will potentially form.

Marvin decided to space the suspenders so that they were not positioned on the nodes of the bridge span. He determined the exact points on the scale model, then he just moved the suspenders a couple of inches over to avoid the nodes.

Jeep tests the gallop on the bridge in 2011.

Chapter 7

The Final Design

Once the suspenders were figured out, Marvin determined the location and anchor points, otherwise known as the dead-men.

The rule of thumb, if there was such a rule, would be to have a 1-to-1 to 1-to-2-1/4 relationship from post/cable height to a horizontal point back from the post to the dead man position. Marvin opted for a 1-to-1 relationship. Since the posts would be 10 feet high, Marvin drew a line from the post as far out as it needed to be to create that angle to the connection point of the post. This is the spot for the anchor point. This was why it was important to have a clear area behind the posts on either side of the creek.

Level spot for the dead-men

32 BUILDING A SMALL CABLE SUSPENSION BRIDGE

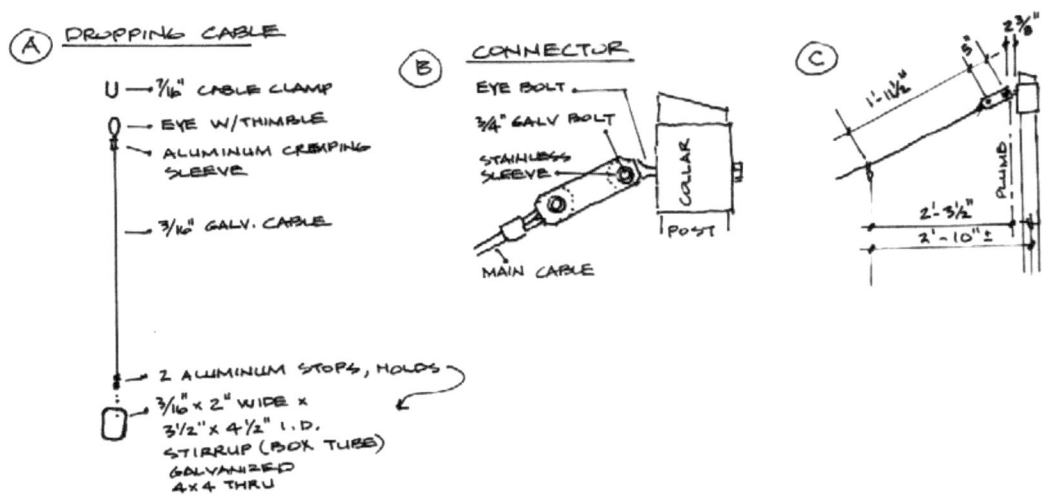

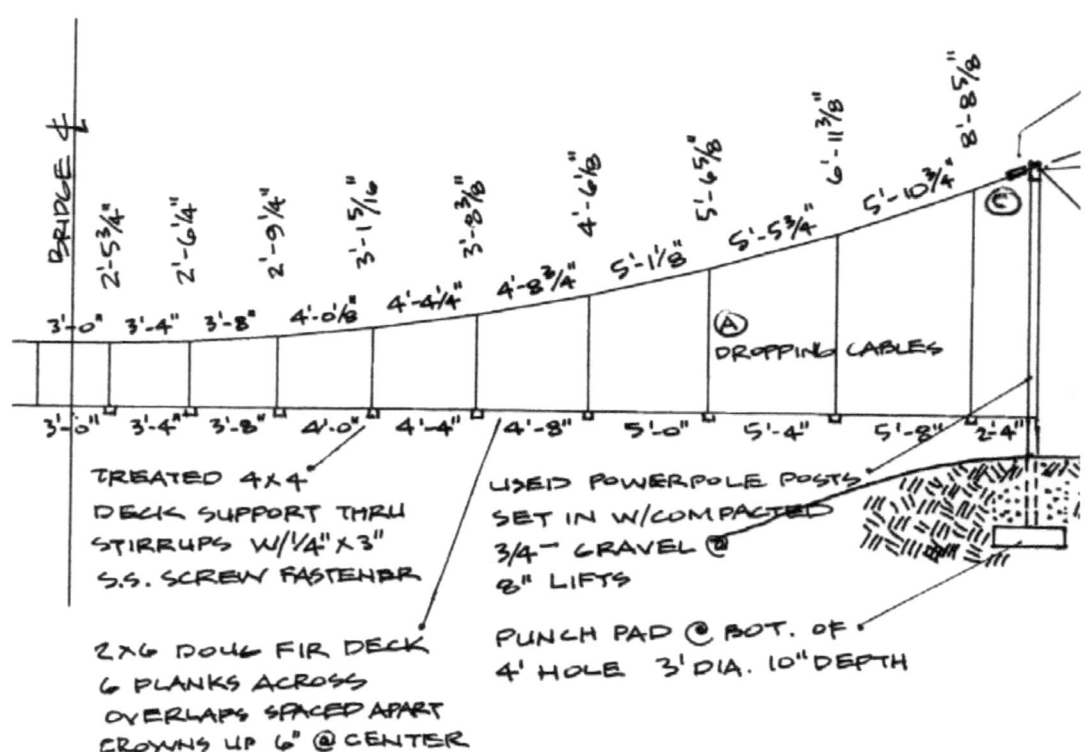

At that point, Marvin just used the scale ratio to determine the final lengths of all the cable parts and drew up the final bridge plan. The planning of all the parts was integral in creating this bridge. The deck would eventually be built on the fly, sort of like a LEGO® kit, so having all the components cut to fit accurately was important.

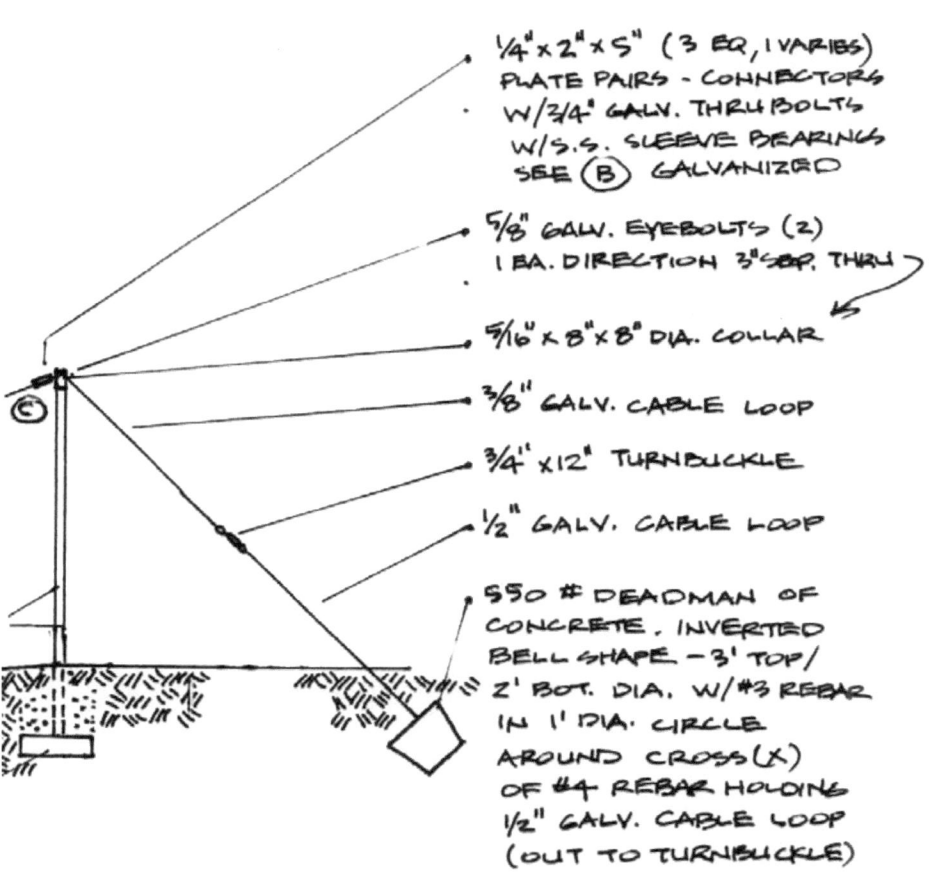

34 BUILDING A SMALL CABLE SUSPENSION BRIDGE

There are a lot of ways to build a bridge like ours. Sometimes, holes are drilled through the deck beams and cable or rope running through the beams is spanned across the chasm and secured to the posts on either side. This design is not only difficult to build on the fly, it is not easy to replace the deck beams if they rot or are damaged in some way.

Sometimes, suspenders hang from the main cables such as in Marvin's design, then through holes in the deck beams to be knotted or secured in some way underneath. Eye-hooks are also used to secure the suspender to the deck beam. While this design could be built on the fly, maybe a bit awkwardly, again there is the issue of the difficulty in replacing rotted or damaged beams.

Marvin's design, using the "cable locking system," allows for both easier installation, using minimal tools on-site, and effortless replacement of the deck beams.

This suspension bridge has the deck beams bolted to the cables.
Photo by Zastol`skiy Victor Leonidovich/Shutterstock.com

Chapter 8

Getting Started

Building this bridge was pretty much a one-man show with a woman to buy the donuts (and write the book). We also had a helpful friend named Doug who chipped in when needed. Doug was happy to help with such an interesting project.

Meanwhile Marvin came up with a lot of tricks and ideas to help make the job pretty easy for one or two people to accomplish. The cable-locking system had a lot to do with the ease of building the bridge, but the way Marvin accomplished the foundation and cable construction was pretty impressive for a guy without much power equipment to assist in the tasks.

Getting back and forth across the creek was a tricky task.

First, Marvin spent a lot of time clearing the site. Both sides were thick with blackberry, nine bark, and salmonberry. The site he chose had plenty of trees, but none in the way of the post sites or dead men sites. A grubbing hoe and machete took care of all the brush.

After the brush was cleared away, Marvin laid out the location of the posts and dead-men and double-checked the measurements on everything with the transit and string. Finally, it was time to dig.

There were a total of eight holes to be dug for the project that would house four posts and four dead-men. Marvin started with the postholes. The posts were going to be three feet into the ground, but the plan also called for concrete punch pads, so that meant another ten or so inches of hole to dig.

Top: looking north
Bottom: looking south

Why a punch pad? A two foot wide pad of concrete would help to distribute the weight. The posts were bearing much of the weight of the loads.

If Marvin just set the post to the ground, the point load might exceed the bearing capacity of the native soil. If there were a big load on the deck, such as a tree that fell on it, the posts could sink into the ground and cause the bridge deck to be lower over the creek. The point load would be far less than if he distributed the weight in a concrete pad.

Marvin used a tamping-bar to pry up a few roots that were in the way of digging.

Marvin figured 1,500 pounds of bearing load per square foot, so three square feet of concrete pad totaling twelve square feet would allow for a pretty hefty weight capacity. He also planned to make the pads about ten inches thick to give them more tensile strength in order to prevent cracking.

Meanwhile, the plan also called for backfill with 3/4 minus gravel, which would be tamped at regular intervals. The gravel would help to protect the posts from insects and water damage, plus it would help hold the posts more firmly in the ground.

To allow for the backfill, the holes needed to be about two feet in diameter. Marvin set to work and soon discovered that digging a hole that was only two feet wide was awkward to work in. After digging the first 18 inches or so, he connected the two post holes, creating an oval around both of them. It was easier to work in, plus, there would be that much more gravel backfill to add more security to the posts.

Marvin worried that things might change once the posts were set up, so he decided not to dig the dead-men holes until the posts were in place.

We always use ready-mix concrete for small projects like these punch pads. The bags have the correct ratio of sand, gravel, and cement in them, so all one has to add is water and an energetic mixer. Some people don't even bother to mix, but if you want a strong concrete base, you will want to mix it well.

We needed to mix about three cubic feet of concrete for each punch pad, which amounted to six bags of 60 lb. ready mix per hole. Rebar and drift pins were already set into place. The pins stuck up about two inches from the center once the pads were poured. When the punch pads were cured, it was time to set the posts.

Punch pads in place were later covered to prevent injury.

Chapter 9

Setting the Posts

Getting the posts over to the other side was the only thing that required some machinery. We have a 1948 9N Ford tractor that can do no wrong, when it runs, which is usually.

A post was secured to a cable that was then passed through a pulley attached to the trees on the opposite bank. With the cable attached to the tractor, Marvin drove the tractor away from the creek and the post headed across.

One post did land a little low on the bank, but a couple of strategically placed planks helped to flip it up and over. It nearly landed in the hole!

Posts being cabled across the creek.

The logistics of placing the posts was a little tricky. We had two-foot wide holes that were about four-feet deep, a rebar pin sticking up in the middle of each punch pad, and about a 15-foot long 10-inch diameter heavy post to install. Just plunking them in a hole would not have been that difficult, but each post had a hole drilled through the bottom that would meet up with the rebar drift pin. We needed to position each post right over the pin before letting it go.

A few strong people could have probably done it. But even with a bunch of help, the possibility of losing grip on a post and wrecking the sides of the hole was a consideration. Not to mention that we don't know that many strong people.

Marvin built a tripod for placing the posts in the holes. He used three 2x4's that were each 20 feet long. He tied them all together by drilling a hole through the tops and running a flexible cable through all three. This method allowed the 2x4's to be adjustable when placed over the holes.

A 20-foot tall tripod helped to hoist the heavy posts into the holes where they met up with the pins at the bottom.

He placed the towering tripod over a hole, then with a block and tackle attached from the center of the tripod, he noosed a post with the rope. He hoisted the post safely above the hole so he could gently lower it down in place. It was a two-person job, but only to keep the post from swinging against the sides of the hole while someone worked the block and tackle.

Marvin braced the posts securely in place by nailing boards to them and attaching the boards to stakes in the ground. He made sure they were plumb, which was something he checked often during the bridge construction.

Here is Marvin hoisting one of the posts, then securing both with bracing.

Chapter 10

Collars and Backfill

While the golden gate bridge cables pass over the towers and down to the anchor points (drawing on the right), Marvin's suspension bridge design called for a heavy-duty metal collar with a big eye bolt going through each post (drawing on the left). The anchor cables and the main bridge cables would attach to eye bolts on either side of the collars. The reason for using this method was to help stabilize the posts. If weight were applied to the deck, the dead men cables would help hold them in place.

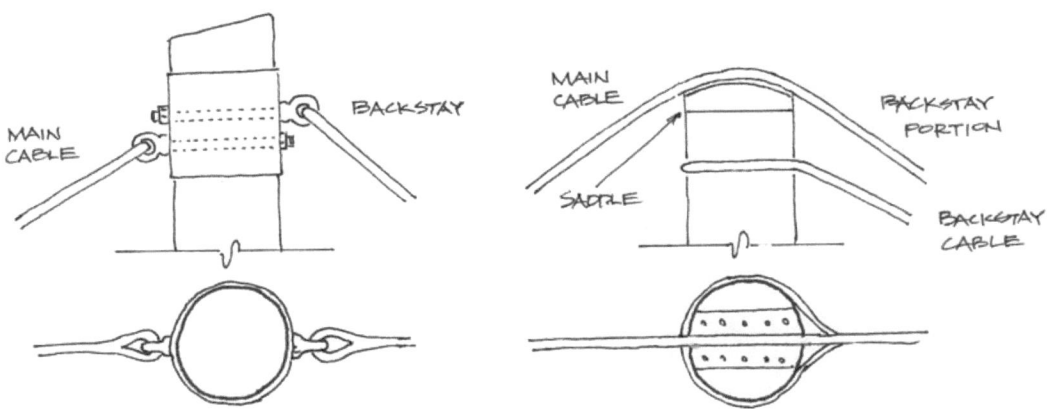

In the golden gate design, the towers would need to be buried a lot deeper and made much more stable in the foundation in case of serious stress on either main cable. Marvin figured he'd get the same look but a stronger, easier to build bridge.

Marvin bought 1/4" thick metal pipe that would fit over the posts. He drilled two holes for eye bolts on opposite sides which lined up with each other.

The fit of the collars was so tight that Marvin chiseled the tops of the posts and made a neat ridge on which the collars would rest. He also painted the collars with a rustproof metal paint before he wiggled them into place on the posts.

It was important to site all four collars so that the connections for the bridge cables were exactly the same height. Once they were finally set into place and lined up with each other, Marvin installed cross members on either side of the collars to keep things secure while the posts were being backfilled with gravel. These cross members would later serve to help stabilize the post and cable system.

It was time to backfill the post holes with gravel.

Collars are set and secured with bracing between the posts.

Marvin calculated that probably about two yards of 3/4 minus gravel was going to be needed to fill in all the post holes and the area between them. He had the gravel dumped close to the bridge site and spent about a day wheel barrowing and shoveling and tamping every six inches.

Soon the posts on one side of the creek were set into place. Now it was time to get to the other side with several hundred pounds of gravel.

Usually both sides of a bridge side are accessible by machinery and human power. This bridge construction, and any bridge being erected from an accessible site to a site that leads to nowhere, can pose some problems when it's time to transport materials.

Transporting about two yards of gravel across the creek would require a lot of creek-crossing with buckets of heavy gravel. One would have to climb down the bank on one side, make the precarious trip across the creek, then scramble up the steep bank with about 40 pounds of gravel.

Marvin came up with an easier way to get the job done.

Braced posts on the far side of the creek are ready for gravel backfill.

Thanks to one of our secure posts on one side and a big tree on the other side, we had just the right set up for a zip line to transport buckets of gravel across the creek.

Marvin constructed a cable and pulley system where a bucket could be hooked up and then zipped across the creek for someone to grab on the other side. Geometry proved that we could not get much of a slope without the bucket slamming into the bank or without hoisting the bucket of gravel beyond the height of the post. So a little extra roping was needed.

Marvin attached rope to the pulley that could be used from either side of the creek, one end for pulling over, the other end for pulling back. That way, when the bucket decided to hang up somewhere over the creek, the helper on the other side could give it a tug. When it was time for the bucket to go back, it could be retrieved easily.

It helped to have our friend Doug standing on the ladder by the post to fill the bucket with gravel and send it over to Robin. She would unhook the bucket, pour the gravel into the hole, and then hook up the empty bucket to the cable for Doug to pull back across the creek.

Doug would latch the bucket hook to a stay hook so the bucket couldn't get away, and Marvin would fill another bucket with gravel and hand it up to Doug. Doug would then pour the gravel in the bucket and unlatch it.

Doug, in the photo below, lifts the bucket to the pulley and sends it across the creek.

Zoom! The bucket would usually zip across the creek. If not, Robin would pull it over using the rope.

Once Robin had poured about six inches of gravel, Marvin could come across the creek to tamp it in while Doug and Robin took a break!

At some point we calculated how many buckets it took to fill the space six inches deep so that Marvin could come over and tamp. We figured about 20 buckets of gravel per six inches, and we had about 48 inches to fill. 160 or so? All we remember is that it was a lot of buckets!

One bucket filled with gravel weighed about 40 pounds

Chapter 11

The Dead-Men

The next project was the dead-men. These anchor points were an integral part of the strength of the bridge, so they really needed to be done properly. Marvin determined the amount of concrete needed, but how to form up for each anchor wasn't worked out yet. He considered using plastic barrels, but decided on large plastic planters instead. They were each about 24" wide and 24" deep.

```
         LOAD CALCULATIONS
   DEAD LOAD
     MAIN CABLES    2 @ 80' x .52#/L.F.        83
     SUSPENDERS    34 @ 6' AV. x .08#/L.F.     16
     STIRRUPS      34 @ 1# ea.                 34
     4x4 BEAMS     17 @ 5'  x 3.83#/L.F.      326
     2x6 PLANKS     6 @ 80' x 2.57#/L.F.     1234

   LIVE LOAD
     PEOPLE         5        x 200# ea.      1000

                         TOTAL              2693 POUNDS
```

Once filled with concrete, each would have about 500 pounds of concrete plus about 20 cubic feet of soil on top which amounted to another 1,000 pounds. That meant the four dead-men could handle about a 6,000 pound load. The dead load of the materials amounted to very little, and a typical live load would be 3-5 people walking across the bridge. And maybe a dog or two. Not even close to 6,000 pounds of load!

But, there was another live load possibility: a tree falling on the bridge. We have some dead western red alders that tower high over the site and a number of live trees that won't live forever. From a height of about 40-60 feet, one of them, or even a hefty branch slamming down on the deck would be a significant impact on the bridge. So Marvin tried to allow for the unexpected as well.

He dug the four holes at a 45 degree angle, making the holes pretty close to the size of the planters but about 24 inches deeper than their depth. Each of the dead-men were to be set at about a 45-degree angle for the cable to run down from the posts. But, since they were at this angle, a system needed to be in place that would keep the concrete from pouring out.

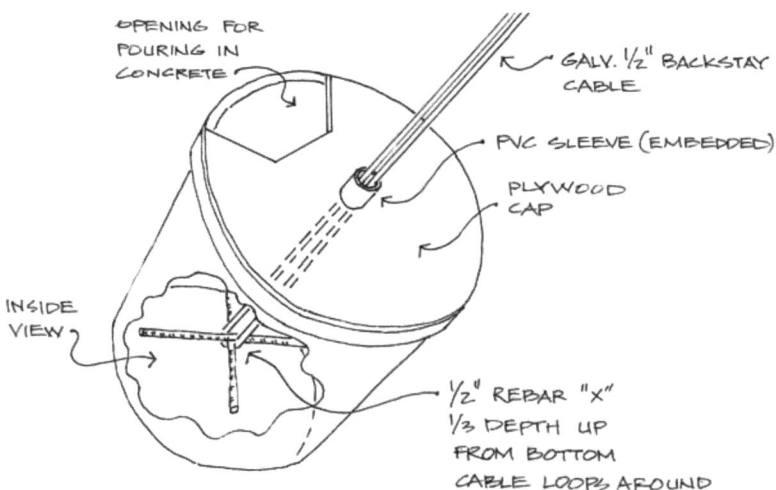

Marvin built tight fitting plywood lids for the planters. He cut a hole in the middle for a piece of pvc pipe that would serve as a sleeve. A loop of 1/2" galvanized cable was inserted so the loop stuck out of the concrete about five feet. Marvin purchased thimbles that fit over the cable loops. The loops would later be connected to the cables that extended from the posts.

He cut an opening at the top of the lid which was where he later shoveled in the concrete.

Once Marvin poured the concrete into the planters and it was allowed to set up overnight, he removed the wooden lids. Then he shoveled and packed in dirt all around and on top of the dead men. The sleeve around the cable was extended above grade. As mentioned, that extra two plus feet of dirt on top added to the weight of the dead men, adding more dead weight.

The collars with their pre-drilled holes were already in place on the tops of the four posts, so the next step was to drill a hole in each post that went into one collar hole, through the post, and out the other collar hole. Marvin used a block of wood to help keep things perpendicular, but he basically just drilled straight through the post. The hole was large enough so there would be some leeway when the bolt was pushed through.

Marvin sprayed copper napthenate into the holes, which is a wood preservative with little impact on the environment. Then he inserted two 10" X 5/8" eye bolts at opposite directions in each post.

The collars would support the main cables on the bridge side as well as the cables to the dead men on the back side.

Marvin cut four lengths of cable that would run through the eye hooks on the back sides, run through the thimbles, and then connect through a turnbuckle that would allow for adjustment once the main cables were installed.

The cables were put in place and the turnbuckles were installed. Now we had four cable systems that ran from the top of each post and down to the dead men about 14 feet away from the posts. Everything was ready for the next step.

The cables to the dead men were almost ready for the next step.

However, Marvin was concerned that this double cable arrangement could be a problem if one of our resident elk or deer got a horn stuck between the cables. One bull elk that weighed roughly a thousand pounds could potentially wreak havoc to the bridge system.

It was a possibility that we knew could be a reality. Years ago a young bull elk got his antlers tangled up in our high-tension wire garden fence and managed to kill himself in his struggle to get free. He also managed to pull down the entire 50x50 foot fence, posts and all.

Before we hauled poor "Harvey" to the woods for a natural burial (the local fauna had a feast), Marvin cut off his head and buried it in the garden to allow the underground beasts to clean the skull.

That summer, we dug up the skull and hung it up over the doorway to Marvin's shop, as a warning to all elk to stay away! We also built a better fence around the garden. Harvey's skull has provided a home and neat perch for the local bird population.

Harvey the elk hangs outside Marvin's shop as a warning for all elk to stay out of the garden.

54 BUILDING A SMALL CABLE SUSPENSION BRIDGE

To protect the cables that ran from the posts to the dead-men, Marvin purchased non-perforated 3" white plastic drainpipe and cut four pieces to span the cables. He then split each piece down the middle so that he could install them over the cable loop. The drainpipe created a single surface that protected the cable from possible antler tangling. The pipe on the cables is not very pretty to look at, but it should help prevent another deadly accident such as the one poor Harvey had with our garden fence, and help keep those cables from animal damage.

Chapter 12

The Cables

Another area of the creek at flood stage in 1996. That's Wailin', our old borderline collie.

The supporting cables consisted of the two main cables that suspended across the creek and the suspender cables that would run from main cable to the bridge beams supporting the deck. Marvin had designed these components on the string model and done all the math. He decided on pre-building the main cables with suspenders away from the bridge site in our pasture nearby. He would set up the cables and suspenders as they would ultimately be implemented in the final cable assembly. The pre-bridge assembly would be much easier to manipulate on land than suspended about 15 feet above the creek bed.

The first cable was laid out accurately and marked with colored tape to note the locations for the suspenders. The second cable was laid out so that it was identical to the first cable.

The main cables needed some good, strong connections on each end. Marvin had a crimping tool for the suspender parts, but we did not own the industrial size crimping tool that was needed for these vital connections. He had the cables crimped by the cable company, where they crimped the two ends of each length of cable so that Marvin had a good size loop to work with. Unfortunately, one cable was about two inches shorter than the other. The cable company people were not used to a precision job, since most of their work did not consist of matching parts. Making two matching equal length cables is not what most cable companies do.

Having one cable shorter than the other was one problem. Marvin also realized that the cables could twist. This could cause a problem when attaching the suspenders.

Marvin created four shackles that would lock the cables into position so that they couldn't twist. This would help the suspenders to line up vertically in a consistent manner.

The collars in place with the shackle connection on the bridge side.

Each shackle was made from two flat plates of 3/16" steel having two holes drilled through each. A bolt was inserted through one hole of the first plate, then through a stainless steel sleeve acting as a bearing that helps prevent wear to the bolts and eyes. The sleeve then fit through the bolt eye on the post and the bolt went through the opposing hole on the second plate. It was nutted and tightened securely.

  A second bolt, also equipped with a stainless steel sleeve, would be installed the same way on the second set of holes to attach to the main cable. One of the four shackle pairs was longer to accommodate the cable that was too short.

Close up showing how the shackle connection attaches to the collar.

Now it was time to put it all together for the test drive. Marvin planted a couple of 4x4 posts in the pasture that were the right distance apart and tall enough to emulate the actual bridge. He hung the main cables from the shackles, which were attached to the two temporary posts. Then he worked on adjusting the two cables to match each other perfectly. The next step was to attach the suspender cables.

The suspenders were cut a bit longer than the plan called for to allow for more tweaking. Marvin slid a metal thimble on each suspender cable and two long sleeves, then curved the cable end through the sleeves and crimped it tight. The thimble would help keep the cable from slipping when it was crimped and help to create a uniform eye.

Suspenders are organized by length then attached to the main cables in a pasture pre-assembly.

The process was a little tricky and took a few trials to figure out just how much slack to leave in order to get a nice eye without pinching the cable or crushing the thimble. He crimped the top sleeve first, then the bottom, being careful to keep both sleeves lined up.

The other end of the suspender needed a stop sleeve. This was an integral part of the cable locking system. The top of the stop needed to be the exact length of the suspender when it was installed into the locking system.

Marvin laid the suspender on a board with a nail on one end and a clamp on the other. He made a mark for the length on the board as well. He slipped on the stop sleeve and got it in position as he clamped the cable so that it was straight.

Marvin found that the sleeves had a tendency to want to creep when being crimped. Crimping slightly got them to stay put, then he could use a hammer to adjust them into position before the final crimp. He added a second stop sleeve for security. Finally, he used a grinder to cut off the excess cable below the stops.

Marvin had considered just crimping the suspenders into their proper positions, but realized that one issue was the inherent twist on a cable. He wanted the suspenders connected tightly to the main cable so that there would be no slippage, but he wanted it to be easy for them to be positioned straight to the bridge deck connections. While the addition of the bridge deck parts would bring them into vertical, he wanted the suspenders to hang straight and true. This would make for a better support system.

Marvin used small U-bolts for the task of connecting the suspenders to the main cables. He connected each bolt to a suspender into its proper place on the cables. The U-bolt had two threaded ends that fed through the suspender eye and a saddle on the top side of the main cable. Tightening down the nuts caused the saddle to squeeze tight on the eye of the suspender cable. This method not only guaranteed a straight hang, it allowed for easy adjustment if they tended to twist, and gave the opportunity for easy replacement if needed.

U-bolts were used to connect the suspenders. Other kinds of clamps and clips could also have been used.

Having the two main cables hanging right next to each other between the pasture posts helped to make sure everything was going to match up on the final installation at the bridge site. Plus the cables gave the local tree swallow population a place to park their fledglings while they swooped over the pasture picking insects out of the air for the hungry babies.

Once Marvin was satisfied that the suspenders were located and fastened in their proper alignment across the 80-foot span and everything else was fine-tuned, it was time to connect it all to the actual bridge posts.

The bridge site was about 200 feet from the assembly site. We rolled up all the suspenders and taped them to the cable for transport. We stretched the cables between the two of us so they couldn't tangle up during the trip. We hooked a shackle end to the collar of each post by inserting bolts, and attached a nylon rope to the other end of each cable.

Up to now, everything has been pretty easy because our creek was passable during summer. Had we been dealing with an impassable canyon, we'd need a way to get to the other side for the foundation and posts. After all, most bridges are a short cut from here to there.

How would we get the cables attached to the other side if we couldn't just carry them over? A helper on the other side could toss over a rope that was connected to their side with a weight on it. If it was too far to toss a rope, they could use a bow and arrow to get it there. Once a rope was stretched across, the helper on this side would tie the cable to the rope and the helper across the way would haul rope and cable to their side and attach the cables to the posts, making sure not to let the main cables twist around.

We strung a nylon rope through the collar connection on the other side and pulled the cable with the rolled up suspenders across the creek. The loop on the cable end was placed between the remaining two holes in the metal shackle and bolted into place. We went back for the other cable and repeated the process. Once those cables with the attached suspenders and stops were in place, we'd have a bridge soon. It was time for donuts!

Marvin secures the second cable with the rolled up suspenders to the post across the creek.

Chapter 13

The Assembly

The integral part of this bridge construction is the cable locking system, a U.S. utility patent. The cable locking system is easy and straightforward. A metal stirrup has a keyhole drilled through the designated top and a metal plate that fits snugly inside the stirrup has a same size keyhole drilled through it. When put together, the metal plate that fits inside the stirrup is turned so that its keyhole is facing the opposite direction from the keyhole in the top of the stirrup.

Marvin threads a suspender wih the stop sleeve through the metal plate inside the stirrup.

In the cable locking system, cable or any other support such as a rope has an enlarged end that is larger than the small part of the keyhole yet smaller than the large part of the keyhole, such as the stop sleeve on our suspender cable. This end goes through both enlarged ends of the keyholes in both the stirrup and the metal plate, then the two parts are put together with their opposing keyhole arrangements. The holes are drilled so that the small parts of each keyhole are directly centered in each metal piece.

This joining of the stirrup, metal plate, and cable via the keyholes creates a locked connection for the cable.

We had all of the metal parts cut and drilled by metal fabricators, and then we had them all galvanized. There is also a hole drilled on one side of each stirrup for a screw that would help keep the joists from slipping out once they were set in place. The cable locking system would not fall apart, but the joists could potentially slip free without that screw.

The cable locking system apart, then with the cable and stop sleeve connected.

The joists that Marvin used were cut from 4x4 Douglas fir posts that had been treated with Alkaline Copper Quartenary (ACQ). This is one of the modern wood preservatives that replaced the arsenic-based solutions. While better for the environment, the copper in ACQ tends to eat metals that are lower on the base scale. To avoid damage to the metal stirrups, Marvin first painted the treated joists with a latex exterior paint, then attached a bituminous stick-on material on the joist ends that would nest between the wood and the metal. The paint would help prevent chemical leeching, and the bituminous material would prevent contact between the metal and ACQ-treated wood.

Marvin pre-cut and carried the joists and the cable locking system parts to the bridge site. He cut 1x4 material to use for spacers. He also hauled over a number of 2x6 boards that were about six feet long. He would use these as walking planks once the bridge started to evolve.

Marvin begins by attaching the first beam into the cable locking system.

Now for the easy part! Marvin attached one cable-locking system to the first suspender cable, simply by fitting the sleeve stop through the two keyholes as previously described. He attached another cable locking system to the suspender cable across from the first, then he slipped a treated post into both stirrups. The bituminous material made the joist ends fit tightly into the stirrups which once in a while required some help from a hammer.

Once he had the three or four pairs of suspenders he could reach by land set up with joists, Marvin attached spacer boards, which he would install all the way across the bridge. The spacer boards were laid out with the same horizontal measurement as the suspender cable layout. Then he tossed up a couple of 2x6 planks so he had something to walk on.

Joists and cable locking system parts are left at one end of the bridge, ready to be installed.

Then he just worked his way across the 80-foot span, installing the parts in the same way from the planks as he did from the ground. It wasn't long before we had a bridge.

68 BUILDING A SMALL CABLE SUSPENSION BRIDGE

Many small-scale suspension bridges use hardware such as eyehooks or they use cable-through-a-hole system to hang the bridge joists. While more difficult to assemble on the fly, this kind of system can also work well, except if the joist rots or breaks from a tree or other heavy object falling on the bridge.

With the cable locking system, if there is a joist that needs to be replaced, one can just remove a single screw from each stirrup, remove the damaged joist and install a new joist in its place. Except for the main cables, all parts are relatively easy to replace.

Chapter 14

Decking and Details

Marvin preps the deck boards before installation.

Decking was another integral part of the bridge design. If you recall the Tacoma Narrows Bridge disaster, wind could cause potential damage even for this small bridge. While not a serious consideration, we wanted to use a strong metal mesh material such as expanded metal sheets that are used for industrial walkways.

70 BUILDING A SMALL CABLE SUSPENSION BRIDGE

This material would let the wind and rain through the deck and give some rigidity to the deck structure. This material would not have many issues such as algae and moss that a wood deck could present in our wet climate. It would also be easy to walk on with a rough metal surface rather than wood that would be slick in wet conditions.

But money was an issue, so Marvin decked the bridge "temporarily" with more affordable 2x6 Douglas fir decking. He kept the pieces spaced so that water could get through (but not little dog feet) and used screws to secure the decking to the joists.

Once the middle deck boards were secured, it was time to remove the spacers

Marvin used cedar to build small staircases on either side of the bridge. Each has a landing and two steps to the ground and can be moved easily.

The last step was to install the sign that all bridges should have. And then it was time to party!

Photo by Marvin Denmark

72 BUILDING A SMALL CABLE SUSPENSION BRIDGE

This bridge continues to be an ongoing project. Marvin plans to put metal caps on the four posts to help them last a bit longer since they started out as 35 year old power poles. He might also put in some kind of handrail and eventually we'll put in that metal deck.

But first, we have plans to build a second bridge on another part of the creek. It will use the cable locking system of construction, but with the main cables going pretty much straight across rather than using the catenary curve.

Meanwhile we are not the only ones enjoying the benefits of our suspension bridge. Last winter we spotted bobcat prints in the snow close to the bridge. Could a bobcat be making good use of our bridge to avoid swimming across that cold torrent? We set up a motion-sensor camera and sure enough, there he was. We wonder if the bear uses it, too, but haven't got a shot of that, yet.

Chapter 15

The Patent

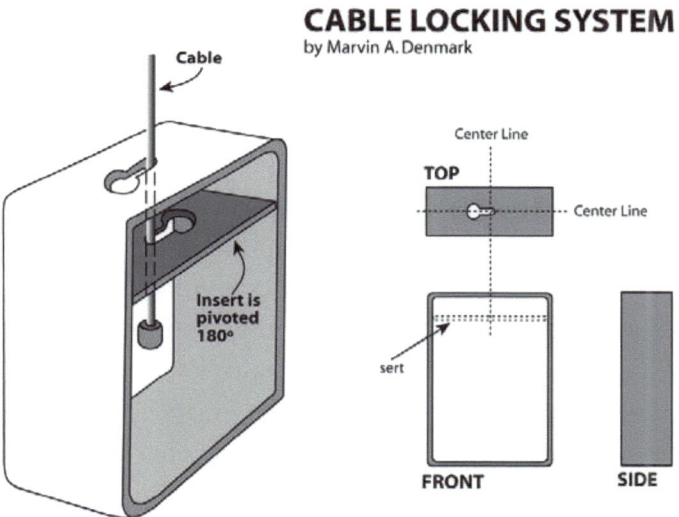

CABLE LOCKING SYSTEM
by Marvin A. Denmark

The title of this book refers to Marvin's cable locking system. When Marvin came up with the bridge design using this method of connecting the suspenders to the deck, we decided to apply for a utility patent.

With no knowledge or experience in patents, we hired a patent attorney to do the initial patent search. They determined that it had never been done, and, it also passed the test for being "unobvious" and therefore was patentable - in their expert opinion.

We knew that hiring an attorney to actually write the patent would cost more money than we had, but when we talked to these people on the phone they assured us that we could write it ourselves and do the drawings and they would charge a much smaller fee to help from that point on.

However, once the search was done, they wanted another $3-5,000 to pursue the patent for us. They denied ever telling us they would simply assist in some capacity. So we told them no thanks and bought David Pressman's book, *Patent it Yourself,* and got to work. It took us a full month to get it all done to the best of our knowledge and understanding of the process.

We wrote a check to the USPTO and sent them our specs, abstract, drawings, and claims - the main components of a patent application. Then we waited about 18 months (which they promise is typical). We did file online so could check in to see if any action had been done. We learned that if we didn't check weekly, the authentication would expire and we'd have to use a recovery code to get back in. Of course, there is no warning that this might happen.

The eighteen months passed and our patent was rejected, with a "non-final" action. Our $500.00 patent search had failed to turn up another patent that the USPTO found and decided was too much like Marvin's invention. Marvin looked at it and said no way, so the games began. We answered with revised claims, and it was rejected again. We filed a continued patent examination (get the book if you want more information) and tried again.

We got some help from the USPTO help-line who assured us that patent examiners are told to help people who weren't using a patent attorney. That is, if we were lucky enough to get someone who was sympathetic.

While our examiner did appear to be on our side, her letters always suggested that we needed to hire an attorney and she didn't seem all that sympathetic. Considering that the attorney we did hire blew it on the patent search, we weren't willing to spend the money even if we had it. Marvin called the examiner and they had a few long conversations. It finally all came down to including the cable in the claims. Without it, our system did not lock.

Finally the examiner agreed to show our new claims to her supervisor. We waited some more, then one morning there was a message on our answering machine from the examiner. Her supervisor had told her she should not have rejected our most recent claim. She offered to rewrite it to include some things she felt needed to be there and then, we'd have our patent. We still have that recording.

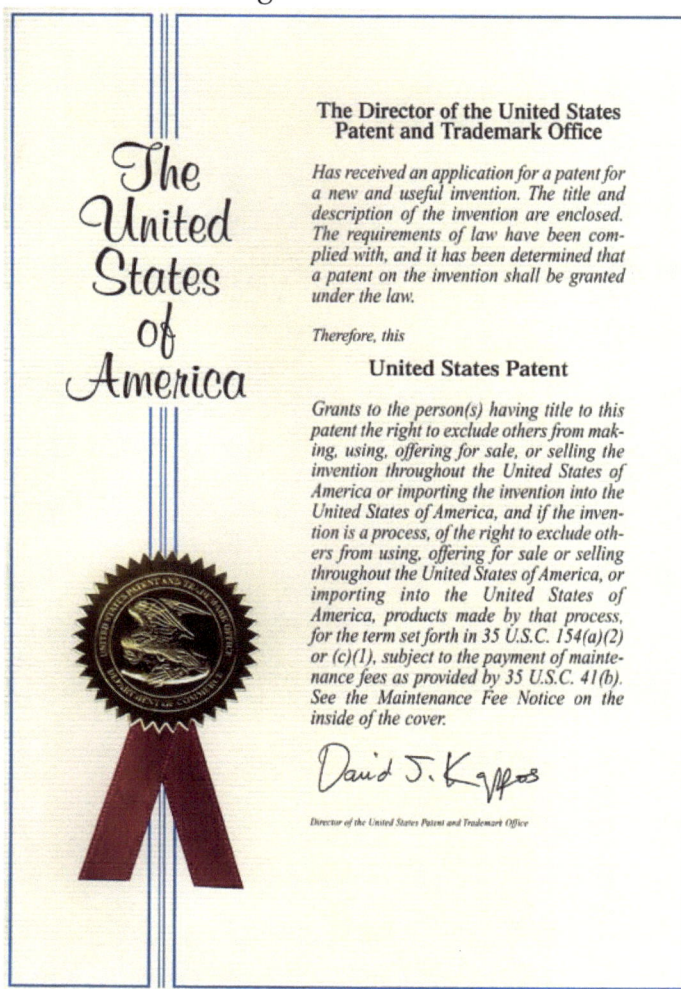

On November 15, 2010, the cable locking system was allowed for a U.S. patent. It took almost three years and about $2,000. An attorney would have cost far more. For instance, had we hired the one who did the search, they would have charged $3-5,000 for the initial patent application. Then when it was rejected for the same reasons ours was rejected, they would have dinged us another several thousand to rewrite it and argue with the examiner. They all have the disclaimer that they can't guarantee the initial patent search is thorough.

All we can say about the entire patent process for the do-it-yourselfer is, "Good luck, and don't give up!"

MATERIALS LIST FOR OUR BRIDGE

Please note that this list applies to our bridge and is for information only; nothing here is implied or intended to be the how-to answer for your particular needs and structural issues. It can simply serve as a general guide to the things you will need if you want to build a bridge like ours, using the cable locking system.

FOUNDATION
Posts
Collars
Gravel
Dead Men containers
Cable parts

CABLE SYSTEM
X feet of ½ inch cable
X feet of ¼ inch cable
Crimping Tool
X Double Sleeves
X Stop Sleeves
X U-bolts

CABLE LOCKING SYSTEM
X stirrups
X inside parts

JOISTS AND DECKING
X feet of 4x4 pressure treated post
X amount bituminous paper cut to size
X screws for stirrups
X screws for planking and decking
X feet of spacing material
X feet of decking/temporary planking

CHRONOLOGICAL LIST OF HOW OUR BRIDGE WENT TOGETHER

- Picked a site, cleared and readied area
- Measured to determine design
- Calculated materials needed
- Designed the bridge using scale model
- Created access across creek
- Dug post foundation holes
- Poured punch pads with drift pins
- Planted posts using tripod assembly
- Plumbed posts and braced for backfill
- Backfilled with ¾ minus gravel, tamping every six inches
- Installed collars on posts and added bracing
- Dug dead men holes
- Poured dead men with cable hook in place
- Hooked up cables from posts to dead men
- Manufactured suspenders using crimping tool
- Mocked up bridge and attached suspenders to main cables
- Installed cable system on posts
- Attached cable locking system and joists
- Screwed cable locking system to joists
- Attached spacers
- Completed bridge span
- Screwed on decking, removed spacers
- Built steps on each side
- Partied!

Afterwords

When I first decided to build a bridge across the creek and realized that the road bridge idea wasn't practical at the time, I saw a neighbor's little footbridge that he had built. That motivated me to build one for our property. I liked the look of the suspension bridge and wanted to try some different approaches in the design and construction.

What I did want was a bridge that kind of looked like the Golden Gate only in much smaller scale. It was all somewhat whimsical, but it had a good purpose. And the bridge idea started out to be a bridge somewhat larger, to get a riding mower across. Hence it became, and remained, wider than was necessary for a walking bridge.

I didn't do research prior to starting, though I don't recommend that. I have a tendency to jump into things without really worrying about how hard it will be or how much time it might take. I've always felt that those things didn't matter as much as doing something new and interesting. It's a challenge and sometimes trial and error, and it did help that I had been solving a variety of building puzzles for a lot of years. And I also don't worry if I know all the answers before I dive into a project. I feel like I will discover the answer by the time I need to accomplish the puzzle at hand.

Having completed the bridge and gotten into the process of writing a book about it all, we found or were given information that could be useful to people who want to build a bridge, in addition to the information we have offered here. There is nothing wrong with researching before starting, even if I don't do it.

One resource we found has some great ideas, from the War Department (January 1944): *Suspension Bridges for Mountain Warfare* - www.fs.fed.us/eng/bridges/documents/susbrdg/warfare.pdf.

This book covers all aspects of building a suspension bridge. The military provides information on suspension bridges for both people or people with equipment, so the bridges are quite stiff. The style doesn't change from equipment to person type. And it is a little heavy and complicated if just building a person type.

But there is much to be taken from the book: 1. They have taken into account all of the safety issues. 2. All of the tasks are set out and organized. 3. All the materials and man power are listed. 4. The details of each part of the bridge are illustrated and the assemblies are explained. 5. All the planning is there; just follow it step by step.

The book could also be a good tool to plan out a different type of suspension bridge. One could borrow all the good ideas presented and apply them to their own take on the suspension theme. Additionally, one could seek out tables showing cable strength for given size that could be useful when deviating from the book.

And here is an interactive website about the hanging cable arch that might be useful when calculating reaction forces on cable supports: http://acg.media.mit.edu/people/simong/statics/data/hangingCableApp.html.

I plan to build another bridge on the property at another spot what will also be a suspension bridge. This bridge will have a much smaller sag in the main cable resembling more of the "jungle vine bridge" style. The walkway deck will probably be only 16-18 inches wide. Otherwise it will employ most of the same ideas in the first bridge, including the cable locking system.

If you decide to use the cable locking system and need the parts, just contact us through our website: www.cablelockingsystem.com or contact me at marvinad@madenmark.com.

Marvin A. Denmark, June 2011

www.ingramcontent.com/pod-product-compliance
Lightning Source LLC
Chambersburg PA
CBHW042029150426
43199CB00002B/11